art by Sinahi Ortega-Hernandez

STOUT FIELD ELEMENTARY SCHOOL

Year (and Coloring) Book

2018

designed by
Stephan Loy

STOUT FIELD STAFF

Mr. Wickard, Principal

Ms. Burchett

Mr. Chope

Mr. Irvine, Vice-principal

Ms. Coe

Mrs. Crimmins

Mrs. Dombrosky

Mrs. Foster

Mrs. Foust

Mrs. Freund

Ms. Garrett

Mrs. Genatiempo

Mrs. Gerbick

Miss Goddard

Mrs. Gomes

Ms. Gray

Mrs. Guajardo

Ms. Hamilton

Ms. Hendricks

Ms. Howard

Mrs. Jarvis Ms. Lakin

Mr. Loy Mrs. Mabus Ms. McIntosh Ms. Miller

Mr. Modglin Mrs. Morris Mrs. Navarro Mr. O'Day Miss Ortiz Ms. Pickett

      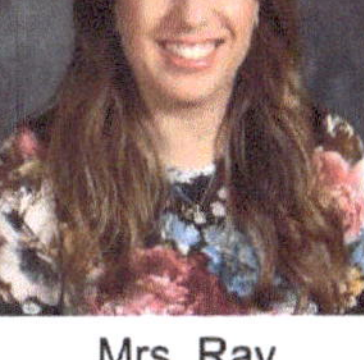

Mrs. Preusch Mrs. Ray Mr. Robbins Ms. Stark Mrs. Stepusin Mrs. Vogt

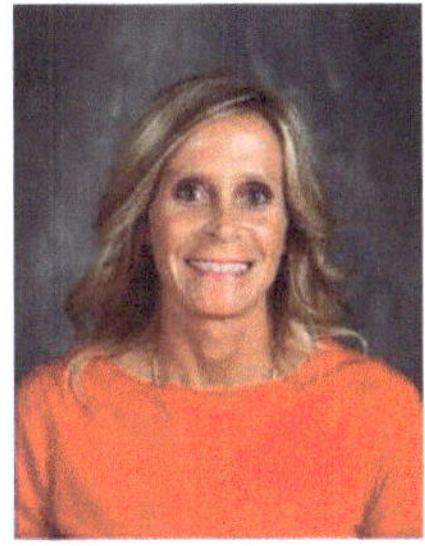   

Nurse Walker Mrs. Walters Mr. White Mrs. White

READING

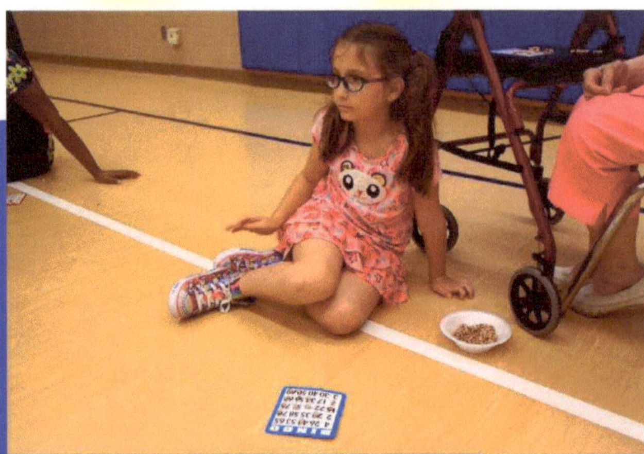

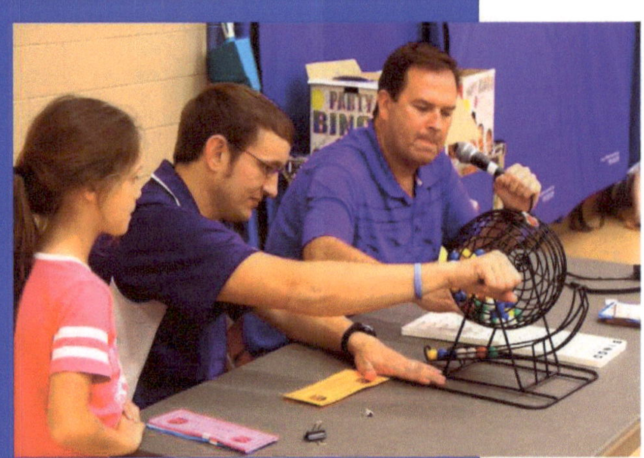

CELEBRATION!

Mrs. Gardner
Pre-Kindergarten

NOT PICTURED:
Christopher Rodriguez

Mr. Cochran
Kindergarten

NOT PICTURED:
Ivyonna Anderson
Raiden Cordero-Herring
Salma Gonzalez
Antoinique Mitchell
Anakin Stone

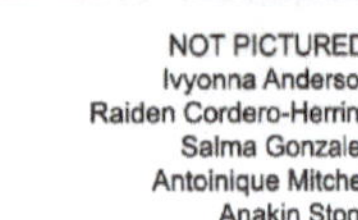

Karter Slayton
Ja'den Wise

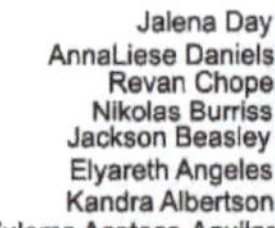

Mrs. Sequin
Kindergarten

Joseph Solgot
Lucas Sparks
Kierston Walker

NOT PICTURED:
Bella Espada
Zion King
Braxton Stanko

Kelly Arguello-Tobar
Bailyn Arthur
Aliyah Beckom
Keegan Cavallero
Kaylee DeBlase Smith
Sofia Gonzalez
Bra'Yonna Harrison
Colton Hoyt

Mrs. Frederick
Kindergarten

Lilly Hunter
Layla Hutson-Martin
Mackinze Johnson
Bryson Mann
Oscar Montez
Jeremie Mukeba

Brandon Ochoa
Monserrat Ochoa-Nevarez
Sophia Ocon
Kylin Shaw
Carl Staples

Jayden Torres
Amerie Zavala

NOT PICTURED:
Kegan Cleary
Nevaeh Clements
Salman Kadiye
Jaxon Lynn

Zoey Charles
Karma Cole
Jayden Collier
Kya Craft
Chrislynn Dayhoff
Abel Englert
Khloe Foster
Nevaeh Johnson

Ms. Youngs
Kindergarten

Xavier Johnson
Sebastian Knox
Bentley Kopp
William Martinez
Riann Ramsey
Jacob Reeves

Shelby Rodriguez
Brooklin Rybolt
Gabriel Samples
Jayla Scott
Giulianna Shackelford
Canden Spray

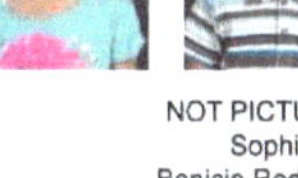

NOT PICTURED:
Sophie King
Benicio Rodriguez

Kinsley Staten
Leah'Anna Stone
Daisy Warner

NOT PICTURED: Braydon Adams, Malil Miller, Gia Morrison-Bryant, Kristopher Spears

Michael Anderson
Zoey Brown
Aleeah Clark
Kloey Cope
Arianna Davidson
Serenity Decker
Kalon Eck
Jayce Foster

Miss Shew
Kindergarten

Kamxin Gehbauer
Michael Greenlaw
Sariah Grimes
James Hall JR
Nivara Honeycutt
Elisea Jackson

James Klein IV
Milow Milburn
Zy'onna Pickerell
Conner Richardson
Kendal Trivett
Semajay Washington

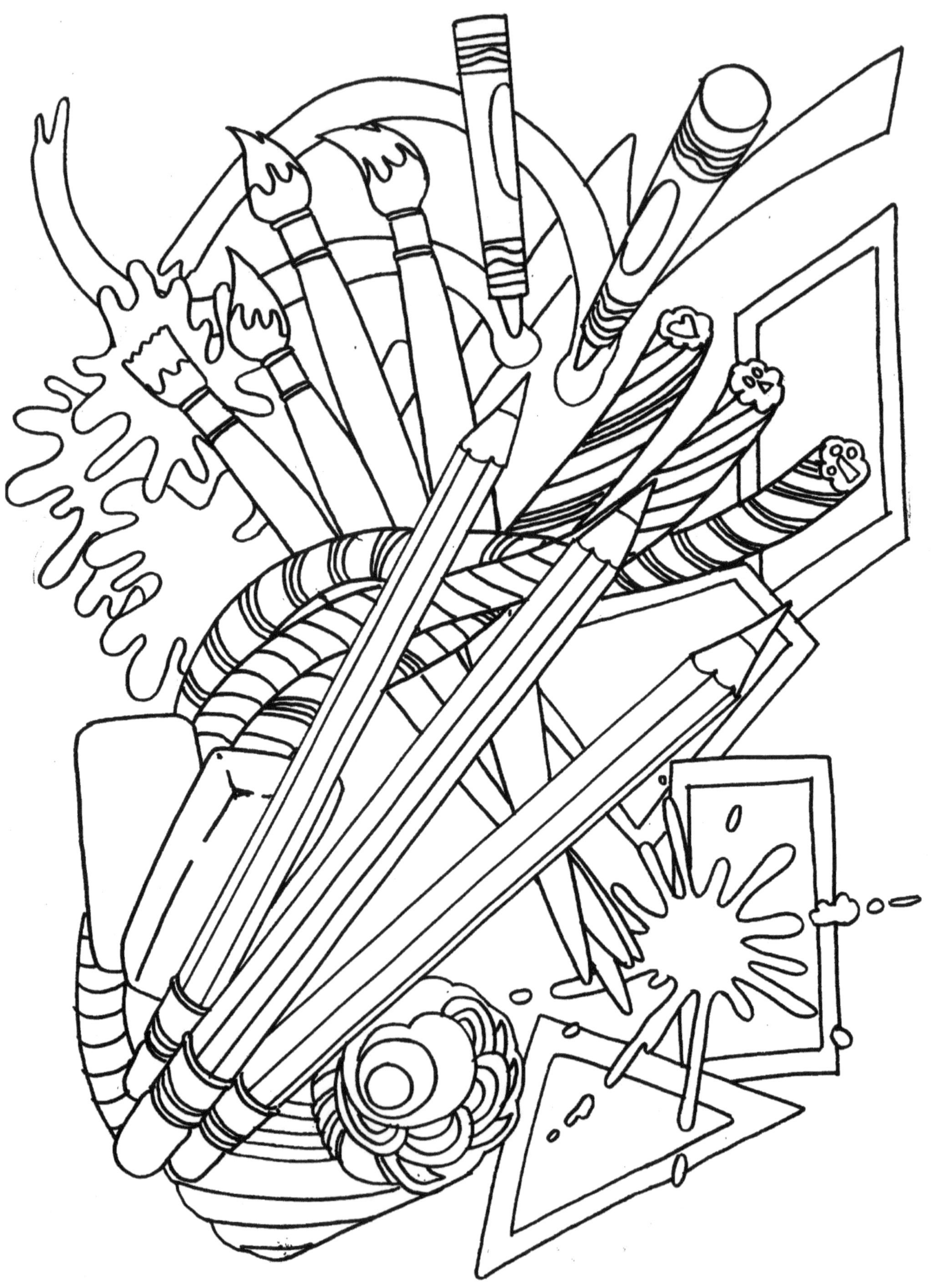

Thomas Banks
Steven Cole
Hannah Coss
Aaliyah DeBlase-Augugliaro
Catori Easley
Payton Garner
Aubree Hawk
Blake Hendricks

Miss Vanarsdale
1st Grade

Caylee Jackson
Elexander Jaimes-Olivia
Darius Knoll
Alayna Lynch
Ryan Manuel
Brayson Matney

Niaylah Medsker
Gregory Phillips
Jason Sanders
Jaylen Sanders
Mary Stone
Megan Stout

William Tiller
Brayden Wheat

NOT PICTURED:
Esabella Kern
Cole King
Santiago Mejia-Pineda
Samantha Prado-Avila
Ivan Quixtiano-Gonzalez

Ayomikun Adewumi
Isabella Atherton
A'myiah Brown
Kamren Cisneros
Gabriella Diaz
Catherine Dorrance-Minch
Helena Funez-Eastridge
Alexa Gallegos-Carrillo

Mrs. Kornbroke
1st Grade

Sophia Garcia
Mia Garcia-Valdez
Llandel Gonzalez
Nohemi Hernandez
Isaiah Ives
Joshua Jones

Crisia Leon-Ardon
Dominick Lovalvo
Jaxon Martin
Christopher Martinez
Sinahi Ortega-Hernandez
Jonathan Perez Ramirez

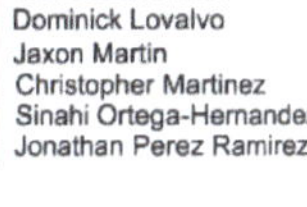
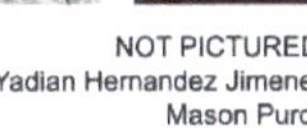

NOT PICTURED:
Yadian Hernandez Jimenez
Mason Purdy

Deon Robinson
Nathaniel Seals
Andrea Villanueva-Serrano
Stevie Willhoite

Lorena Angeles
William Carrico
David Gonzalez
Mahala Harris
Jaylynn Harvey
Ariahanna Lang
Bethany Ledbetter
Malakai Lehman

Mrs. Garner
1st Grade

Brayden Lewis
Myleigh Lisby
Liliana Maldonado
Bentley Mann
Desarai Martin
Helena Moore

Kenny Myers
Toluwani Ogunkoya
Jameson Rayer
Solomon Rodriguez
Jaden Smith
Justyce Starcher

Annabellia Tillberry
Kierra Wells
Gavyn Wood

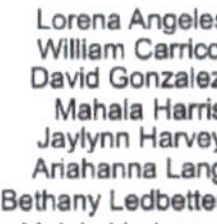

NOT PICTURED:
Jayda Cameron
Angela Mitchell
Clinton Smith
Jozhanae Toliver

Annahbellah Brown
Savouria Browne
Gabriel Cavallero
Alex Curry
Xzavier Elliott
Abril Escobar-Pineda
Saray Hernandez-Merchant
Jayden Kivett

Ms. Kortzendorf
1st Grade

I'Rihanna Lynch
Roy Magallanes-Orozco
Arellys Mondragon-Torres
Makayla Moore
Jack Morris
Peyton Ridener

Alan Rincon
Ismael Romero Avila
Aliegha Scott
Amore Vaughn
Deztinee Vinson
Christopher Zambrano-Jimenez

Lesley Zamora

NOT PICTURED:
Aragon Cordero-Herring
Johanna Martinez
Hailey Massingille

NOT PICTURED: Memori Andrews, Adam Britt, Eric Martinez, Hilse Portillo, Sebastian Russell

Wendy Acateco
Jeffrey Aguiniga
Cortland Doane
Hailie Fuchs
Jesus Garcia
Zofia Gonzalez
Daemyn Harper
Mason Hatfield

Miss Johnson
2nd Grade

Estefania Jackson
Maddy Joerendt
Madelyn Mulvaney
Elijiah Neukam
Carter Norris
Uriel Paz

Luis Quinto
David Rodriguez
Emma Slinker
Jaden Smith
Yahel Tamayo Zetina

Javier Betancourt
Lucy Burriss
Nevaeh Catlett
Damien Cavaliero
Euriah Cowans-Vanover
Makenzy Fink
Alejandro Garcia
Josyah Gilbrech

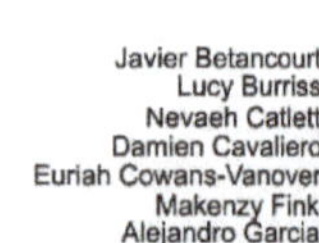

Mrs. Ferguson
2nd Grade

Cameron Griffith
Kamree Henry
Josiah Hower
Logan Lakin
Teona Lang
Aidan Lyons

Jaelyn Manuel
Kayden Martin
Rocco Mediate
Rhiannon Nusbaum
Joseph Rayer II
Christian Robinson

Ian Shultz
Madelynn Taylor
Ethan Warmoth

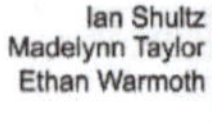

NOT PICTURED:
Aaliyah Clements

Ayomide Adewumi
Penelope Bass
Jazalena Bautista-Hatley
Colton Fox
Kennady Kendall
Sophia Landau
Brian Lopez
Manuel Lopez

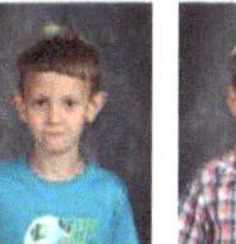

Miss Rudisill
2nd Grade

Geneva Lutzke
Jameson Mercer
Dawson Miller
Haeley Molina
Naomi Monroy-Villeda
Madison Morales

Valarie Morales
Dylan Murray-Tierney
Davion Nard
Ethan Pavey
Chelsea Roberts
Benjamin Santiago

Jayden Spurlin

NOT PICTURED:
Jackie Tindall

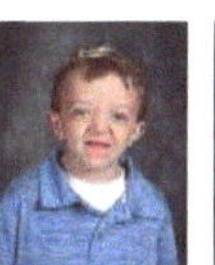

Shyla Boyles
Wyatt Deboy
Brayden Decker
James England
Samson Hall
Jace Hess
Josiah Ives
Israel Lopez-Espinoza

Mrs.Isom
2nd Grade

Madeleine McDaniel
Bentley Mountcastle
Analy Ochoa-Nevarez
Yoselin Perez-Flores
Debrianna Purdy
Nathaniel Quilliam

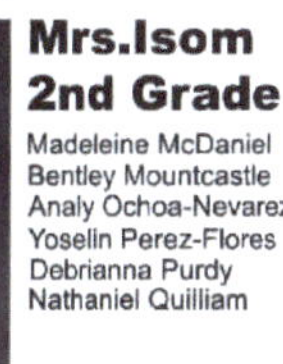

NOT PICTURED:
Michael Anderson
Jossean Argueta Meza
Richard Blanton
Briana Herrera
Blake Smith
Kayleb Stanko

Angelica Ramirez-Alcantar
Alan Rodriguez Valero
Allyson Roman-Lopez
Lesly Terrazas

Bryce Baker
Gavin Ball
Ciera Beck
Juanito Blanton
Ilyssa Collins
Alexander Diaz
Jahnalei Gehbauer
Anthony Grier

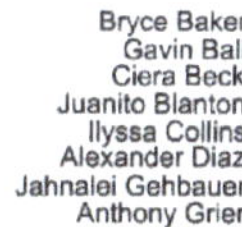

Mrs. Kelly
2nd Grade

Benjamin Grimes
Za'Maria Harrison
Anthony Johnson
William Layton
Daisy Little
Carlos Martinez

Nevaeh McMahan
Chas Miller
AnnaLaya Paschall
Heavenly Radcliff
Jacob Roller
Brent Schmidt

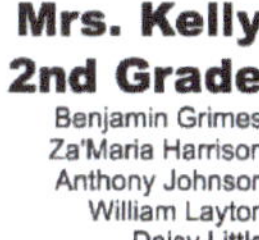

Devan Shelton
Damian Smith
Jessie Wilson
Summer Wilson

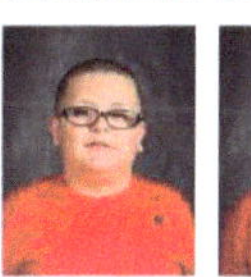

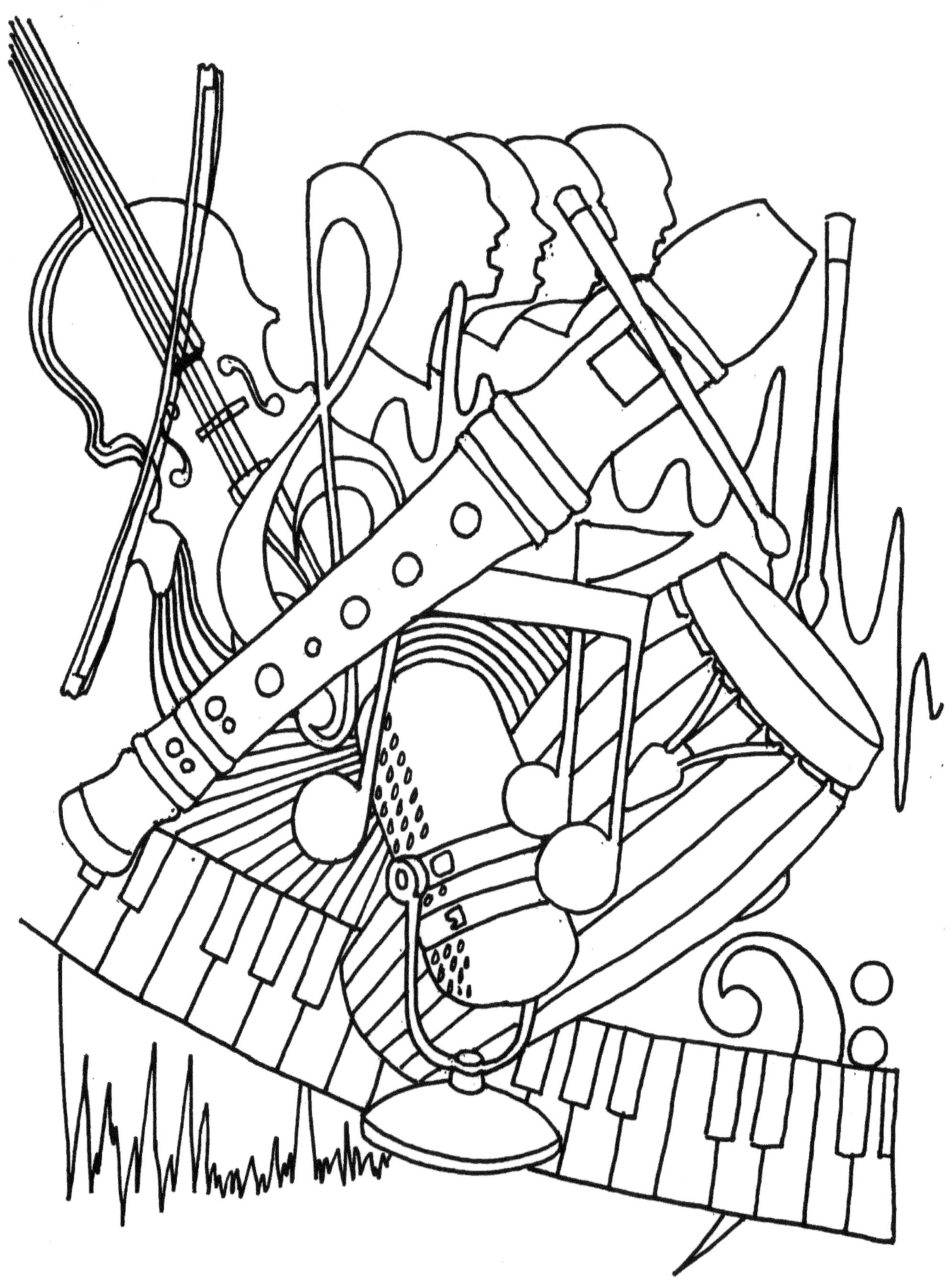

Taiwo Afolabi
Kylynne Bowling
Brandon Brown
Joseph Craig
Alivia DeBlase Augugliaro
Lilah Gebrekidan
Ana-Lucia Gonzalez
Landon Haney

Miss Waire
3rd Grade

Jerome Hardin
Vincent Judd
Mason Keller
Carlee Kirby
Jahleel Lewis
Nataleigh Melton

Kaley Robertson
Brenton Siegrist
Mariah Snodgrass
Alexa Tejada
Amaru Woods

NOT PICTURED: Phailynn Abner, Gracelyn Henson, Tony Matthews, Hailie Sleeth, Robert Stewart

Kayleigh Austin
Gavin Davis
Jase Doane
Jakirra Gilbrech
Miranda Haney
Dylan Hinton
Zachariah Hixon
Chance Jackson

Miss Steiner
3rd Grade

Mackynzie Knowles
Zayden Miller
Khianna Murray-Tierney
Isaiah Myers
Trenati Parsley
Jada-Marie Perry

Thorn Pollard
Nevaeh Pruitt
Gianna Sansing
Bra'eden Totton
Franklin Wade
Ethan Webb

NOT PICTURED:
Trinity Robinson
Brandon Stout

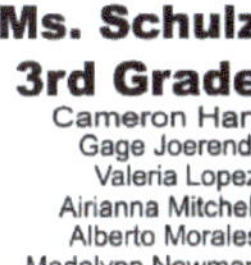

Dereon West
Layla Wirey

Malik Abdulrasheed
Kehinde Afolabi
Landon Allen
Ernest Brunty
Barbara Funez-Eastridge
Miguel Galeana Virgen
Evelyn Gardner
Leila Gebrekidan

Ms. Schulz
3rd Grade

Cameron Hart
Gage Joerendt
Valeria Lopez
Airianna Mitchell
Alberto Morales
Madalynn Newman

Jesse Nobles
Andrew Nunez-Alcantar
Donovin Oliver
Abigail Perez Flores
Miguel Rosa
Keeley Rush

Benjamin Swallow

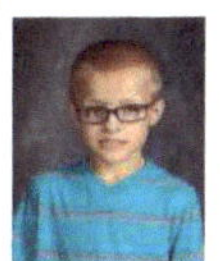

NOT PICTURED:
Perlita Marquez-Caceres
Mariah McMasters
Kory Rucker
Kory Rucker
Summer Sylvia

Sophia Beasley
Adrien Branam
Abril Delgado
Aerith Delgado
Izyah Elliott
Hunter Gay
Alliemae Harris
Elijah Hess

Mrs. Hancock
3rd Grade

Valeria Moreno
Landon Noel
Hadassa Palacios-Estrada
Joseph Perez
Joanna Perez-Ramirez
Anastasia Ramsey

Gracie Ridenour
Conner Rinker
Yaretzi Salinas
Alexis Scott
Timothy Spears
Makenzie Tetrick

David Troxtell

NOT PICTURED:
Dewayne Gregory
Blessing Hill
Karma Phillips

Tessa Alger
Adilson Caceres
Brooklynn Chambers
Gloriann Couch
Jaden Daniels
Alexandra Esparza-Valle
Jackson Gibson
Samantha Gonzalez

Mrs. Evans
4th Grade

Amethyst Judd
Liliana Lobatos Castro
Marco Martinez
Kailani Montgomery
Julian Morrow
Jehobany Murillo

Gavin Palmer
Caidyn Pavey
Emmanuel Paz
Marco Ponce
Andres Pritt
Stephen Repass

Erik Rincon-Munoz
Raquel Rivera-Sells
Taylor Smith
Lee Spencer
Carl Spicer
Omar Xique-Perez
Ricardo Zamora Gonzalez

Sherline Aguila Puebla
Jason Brunes
Gustavo Castillo
Saveahnna Chambers
Divada Charnes
Kalycia Cisneros
Dawson Ferguson
Kaydence Hall

Ms. Guthier
4th Grade

Jesse Hess
Trista Johnson
Bryce Kennedy
Brooklynn Kivett
Sereniti Lawrence
Gracie Luttrell

Ein Macy
Isaiah Matthews
Nolyn Neel
Kayla Perez
Yoselin Rodriguez
Elias Sanchez

Elijah Sandoval
Jacob Shrum
Sevin Tetrick
Eric Tillery
Nehemiah West
Jaxson Willey

Savanna Anderson
Landen Bracci-Cook
Jesslynn Casteel
Jordan Crawford
Lynnae Dalzell
Ricky Fasel
William Gay
Amiah Hamilton

   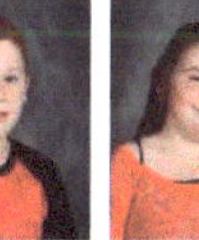    

Mrs. Stuhrenberg
4th Grade

Dylan Janssen
Yancy Li
Mila McGee
Ayisha McNeil
Aeriyona Merrill
Leticia Montes

Benjamin Pugh
Cayden Singer
Lindsey Sterrett
Grace Stone
George Strader
Riley Teepe

Charles Tillery
Joanna Vester
Makayla Wilson

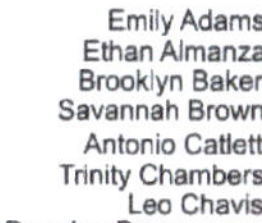 

NOT PICTURED:
Mariah Gonzalez
Dylan Janssen
Emanuel Medrano
Conner Morgan
Lilly Sherwood

NOT PICTURED: Jonathan Davis JR, Xavier Hill, Diego Mallard, Makayla Massingille, Keira Matthews, Ezequiel Monrroy, Alex Norris

Christopher Baker
Fayth Cardwell
Ashlynn Chambers
Kadence Decker
Cody Ellis
Darien Gay
Christina Hardin
Jamir Harper

Miss Lathrop
4th Grade

William Hoskins
Thomas Joerendt
Raymundo Lopez
Ashlyn Lynch
Alexa Mondragon-Torres
Bradley Moore

Tyler Morris
Nevaeh Palmer
Kyler Peebles
Aden Rike
Isabella Russell
Haylee Schmidt

Izeelah Smith
Isaac Swafford
Noah Waites
Kyle Webb
Lillian White

Emily Adams
Ethan Almanza
Brooklyn Baker
Savannah Brown
Antonio Catlett
Trinity Chambers
Leo Chavis
Brandon Dennemann

Miss Hayes
5th Grade

Stephen Fleener
Brendan Fox
Christian Gopar
Sophia Grider
Hayden Grimes
Joshua Landau

Daira Lobatos
David Long
Brooklyn Manning
Dezaray Mingee
Rachel Molina
Ashlye Murillo

Alexis Neice
Joslyn Singer
Kassandra Stafford
Savannah Wick
Lamont Wilson

Career Day

Some of our Superintendant's Award Winners!

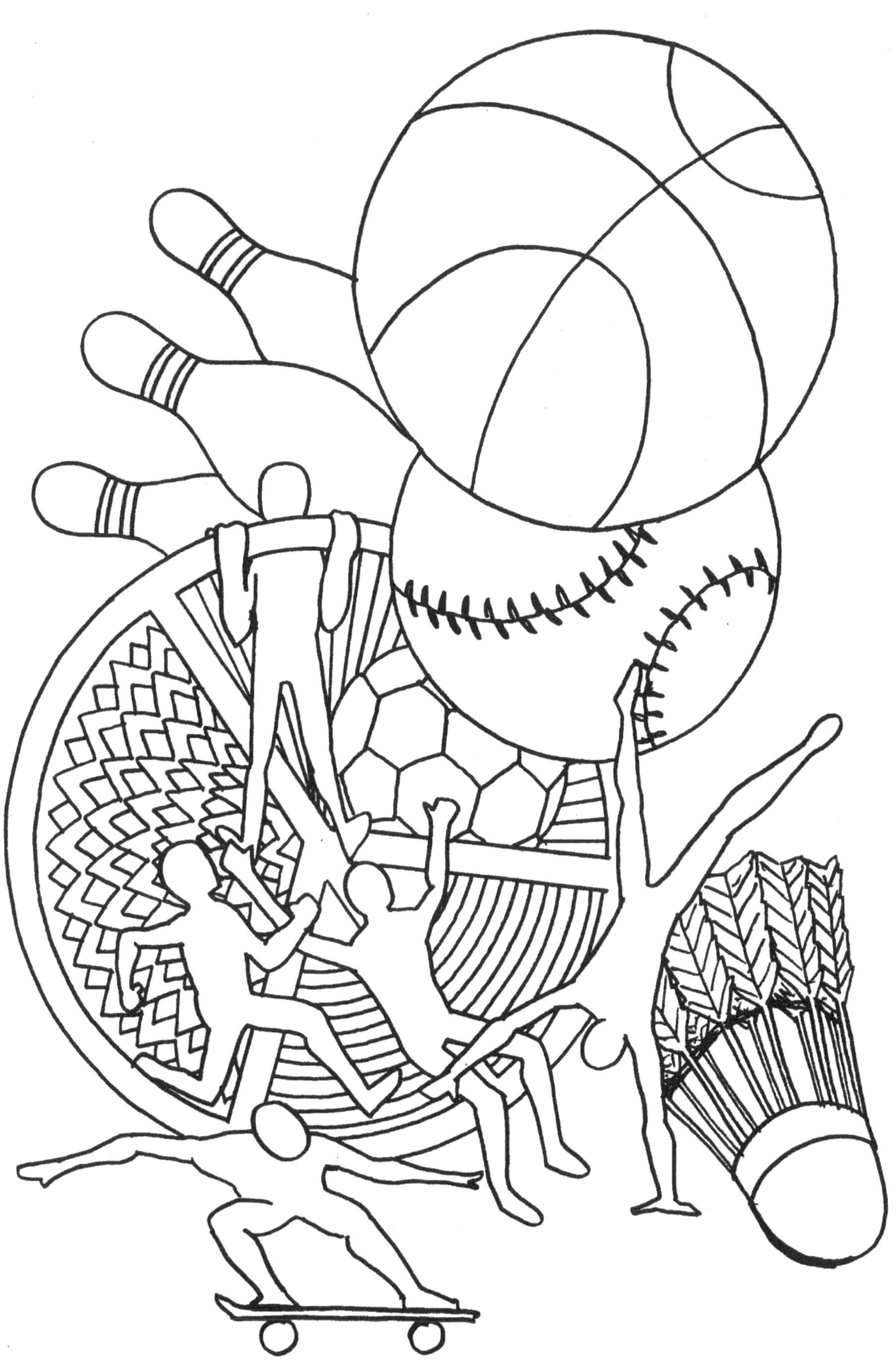

Cleyber Alfaro De Leon
Alana Allen
Bridget Bannister
Thomas Clark JR
Joy Codalata
Jaylynn Davis
Kassandra Dorrance-Minch
Osvaldo Esparza-Valle

Ms. Bluiett
5th Grade

Elizabeth Ferguson
Joselyn Fuentes
Hannah Gay
Nictahet Godoy
Angel Hernandez-Acosta
Vanessa Martinez

Roberto Mazariegos-Leon
Alana Perez
Elijah Ponds
Lindsey Ramos
Omar Santiago
Jalicia Sarden

Alberto Valentin
Ximena Vargas
Dallas Wise

NOT PICTURED:
Kasandra McMasters
Mohamed Osman

Daniel Aguila-Puebla
Briana Bradford
Fredi Campos
Cassandra Carrera
Caitlynn Chambers
Michael Crowder-Lopez
Christian Cunningham
Jeremy DeBoy

Mr. Gilliam
5th Grade

Joselin Diaz
Faith Ferguson
Alondra Fuentes
Simon Gardner
Joaquin Guajardo
Luis Hernandez-Acosta

Dezyrae Joerendt
Jasmine Knowles
Jasmyn Manuel
Ashton Medsker
Rocco Nobles
Eden Pryor

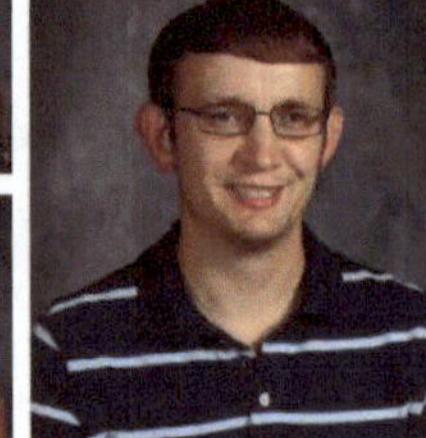

Nicole Rike
Yesenia Rodriguez
Tayler Ross
Alissa Sanders
Orlando Vargas
Damien Wilcox

NOT PICTURED: Cristopher Ramirez Cordova

---

art by Madison Lay

Jazmin Baker
Adam Dalzell
Akiri Davis
Brayden Davis
Thomas Fields
Olivia Fredricks
Hayley Funez-Eastridge
Harlie Gibson

Mr. Duffey
5th Grade

Justin Gilbrech
Alize Jack
Brayden Janssen
Alexia Lockhart
Richard Molina
Avah Nagy

David Palmer
Taniyah Payne
Hailey Pierce
Joseph Post JR
Connor Ramsey
Justin Smith II

Mrs. Thompkins
5th Grade

NOT PICTURED: Dawson Harris, Giovanni Morrison, Amorra Morrow, Alyssa Russell, DeShawn Steinke

---

Mr. Archer
6th Grade

NOT PICTURED:
Robert Garcia
Micah Hawthorpe
Taylor Mays
JoAnn Monrroy
James Smith

art by Mason Albertson

NOT PICTURED: Oscar Ramirez Cordova, Devon Tackett

Mrs. McIntyre
6th Grade

art by Taylor Mays

       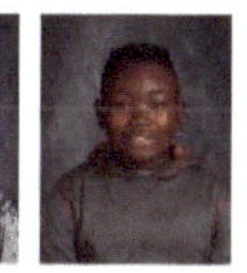 

Dillon Allen
Clarita Boyles
Desiree Chambers
Ronald Cole III
Miranda Edwards
Illianna Erwin
Joseph Flores
Angela Gonzalez

Mrs. Hunt
6th Grade

Jayla Harrod-Wilson
Hannah Hillock
Elizabeth Lang
Lloyd Liscomb
Jaylen Marsh
Kaleigh McCullough

Jordan Miller
Makynzie Myers
Faith Noel
Correll Parson
Owen Reagan
Andrew Rojas

Robert Ryan
Mykell Searcy
Trinity Slater
Darian Smith
Bryce Vinson
Tyah Willhoite

NOT PICTURED: Angel Hernandez-Sanchez, Valerie Tindall, Natalia Vargas

NOT PICTURED: Nevaeh Blanton, Casey Brown, Darling Castillo, Crystal Creek, DeAngelo Gonzalez, Stephanie Gonzalez,

Emma Abner
Oluwajomiloju Akintola
Abraham Bellmore
Brianna Davis
Isaac Eary
Rodney Eaton
Fabriela Gomez-Cruz
Donavan Herron

Ms. Menefee
6th Grade

Jaden Johnson
Baylee Lakin
Chadwick Matthews JR
Keren Mazariegos-Leon
Kaden Neal
Cody Noel

Jacob Perdue
Franklin Portillo
Isabella Servin
William Smith
Madison Sterrett
Vincent Towns

Carol Troxtell
Josie Vester
Kamryn Wesling

art by Summer Wilson

art by Cole King

Winter Music Program

Mystery
HISTORY
fantasy
sci-fi
HORROR!

GROUPS AND CLUBS

Sonic Book Club

6th Grade Student Ambassadors

PE Helpers

6th Grade Morning Announcers

5th Grade Music Helpers

Violin Groups 1, 2, and 3

4th and 5th Grade Girls Run This

6th Grade Music Helpers

Monumental Kids
Movement
Running Club
5th Grade

The Children's Museum Presents...

Treasures of the Earth!

Princess
Choice
Ball

art by Damian Allen Smith

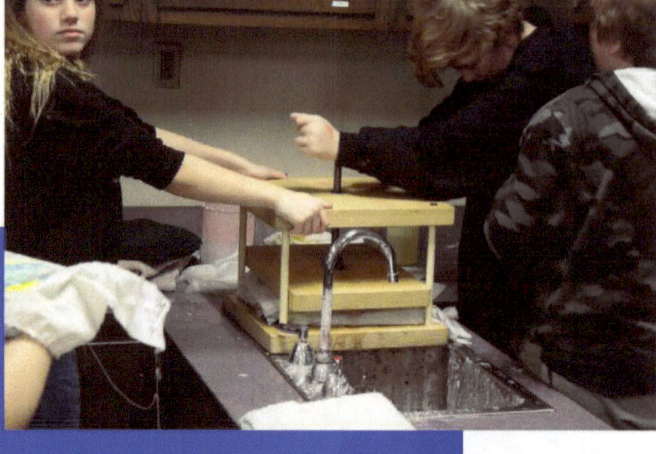

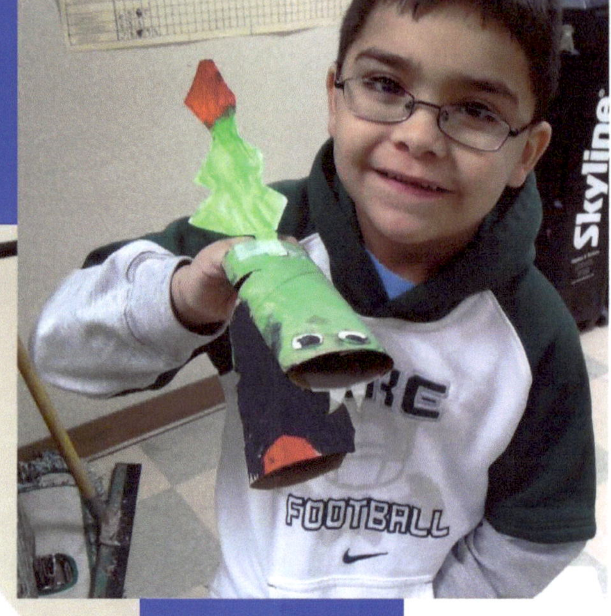

art by Jaden Leclaire

www.ingramcontent.com/pod-product-compliance
Lightning Source LLC
Chambersburg PA
CBHW041135260726
48664CB00027B/1207